50 Mastering the Art of BBQ Recipes

By: Kelly Johnson

Table of Contents

- Classic BBQ Ribs
- Smoked Brisket
- Grilled Ribeye Steaks
- Pulled Pork Sandwiches
- BBQ Chicken with Honey Mustard Glaze
- Grilled Shrimp Skewers with Cajun Spice
- Spicy BBQ Pork Belly
- Smoked Sausages with Beer and Mustard
- Grilled Vegetables with Balsamic Glaze
- BBQ Pulled Chicken Tacos
- Smoky BBQ Meatballs
- Grilled Lamb Chops with Herb Marinade
- BBQ Chicken Wings with Tangy Sauce
- Cedar-Planked Salmon with Maple Glaze
- BBQ Pulled Jackfruit Sandwiches
- Smoked Turkey Breast
- Grilled Corn on the Cob with Chili Butter
- BBQ Beef Brisket Burnt Ends
- Marinated Flank Steak with Chimichurri
- Grilled Portobello Mushrooms with Garlic Butter
- BBQ Baby Back Ribs with Dry Rub
- Smoked Whole Chicken with Lemon Herb Marinade
- BBQ Grilled Shrimp with Garlic Butter
- Grilled BBQ Chicken Thighs with Sweet Sauce
- Spicy BBQ Meatloaf
- Smoked Pork Shoulder with Apple Cider Glaze
- Grilled BBQ Tofu Skewers
- Cajun-Style BBQ Shrimp
- BBQ Sliders with Pickles and Mustard
- Grilled Fish Tacos with BBQ Sauce
- Smoked Beef Short Ribs
- Grilled Honey BBQ Chicken Drumsticks
- BBQ Duck with Sweet Soy Glaze
- Grilled Zucchini and Squash with Smoky Sauce
- BBQ-Style Pulled Beef Sandwiches

- Grilled Pineapple with Brown Sugar Glaze
- BBQ Brisket Tacos with Spicy Salsa
- Smoked Salmon with Dill and Lemon
- BBQ Veggie Skewers with Herb Marinade
- Grilled BBQ Pork Chops with Apple Sauce
- Smoked Brisket Chili
- Grilled Shrimp with Pineapple Salsa
- BBQ Hot Dogs with Spicy Relish
- Grilled Baby Potatoes with Smoky Ranch Dressing
- BBQ Beef Kabobs with Vegetables
- Grilled Shrimp Po' Boys
- Smoked Beef Tenderloin with Red Wine Sauce
- Grilled Cajun Chicken with Avocado Salsa
- BBQ Grilled Flatbreads with Veggies
- Smoked Salmon with BBQ Glaze

Classic BBQ Ribs

Ingredients:

- 2 racks of baby back ribs
- 1/4 cup olive oil
- 1/4 cup apple cider vinegar
- 1/2 cup BBQ sauce
- 2 tablespoons brown sugar
- 1 tablespoon paprika
- 1 tablespoon garlic powder
- 1 tablespoon onion powder
- 1 teaspoon salt
- 1 teaspoon black pepper
- 1 teaspoon chili powder

Instructions:

1. Preheat your grill or smoker to 250°F (120°C).
2. Remove the membrane from the ribs and rub with olive oil and apple cider vinegar.
3. In a small bowl, mix brown sugar, paprika, garlic powder, onion powder, salt, pepper, and chili powder. Rub this spice mix onto the ribs.
4. Place the ribs on the grill and cook low and slow for 2.5-3 hours, keeping the temperature steady.
5. In the last 30 minutes, brush the ribs with BBQ sauce and continue to cook.
6. Serve with extra BBQ sauce.

Smoked Brisket

Ingredients:

- 5-6 lbs brisket
- 1/4 cup mustard (as a binder)
- 1/4 cup kosher salt
- 1/4 cup black pepper
- 2 tablespoons paprika
- 1 tablespoon garlic powder
- 1 tablespoon onion powder
- 1 teaspoon cayenne pepper
- 1/2 cup beef broth (for moisture)

Instructions:

1. Preheat your smoker to 225°F (110°C).
2. Rub the brisket with mustard and coat generously with salt, pepper, paprika, garlic powder, onion powder, and cayenne.
3. Place the brisket fat-side up in the smoker. Smoke for about 10-12 hours, or until the internal temperature reaches 195°F (90°C).
4. Baste the brisket with beef broth every few hours to maintain moisture.
5. Let the brisket rest for 30-45 minutes before slicing.

Grilled Ribeye Steaks

Ingredients:

- 4 ribeye steaks (1-inch thick)
- 2 tablespoons olive oil
- 1 tablespoon garlic powder
- 1 tablespoon onion powder
- Salt and pepper to taste
- 2 tablespoons butter (optional, for serving)
- Fresh herbs (such as thyme or rosemary)

Instructions:

1. Preheat your grill to high heat.
2. Brush the steaks with olive oil and season generously with garlic powder, onion powder, salt, and pepper.
3. Grill the steaks for about 4-5 minutes per side for medium-rare, or longer for your desired doneness.
4. Optional: In the last minute of grilling, top each steak with a tablespoon of butter and fresh herbs.
5. Let the steaks rest for 5 minutes before serving.

Pulled Pork Sandwiches

Ingredients:

- 4-5 lbs pork shoulder (bone-in)
- 1/4 cup apple cider vinegar
- 1/4 cup BBQ sauce
- 1 tablespoon paprika
- 1 tablespoon garlic powder
- 1 tablespoon brown sugar
- 1 teaspoon cumin
- Salt and pepper to taste
- Buns and coleslaw (for serving)

Instructions:

1. Preheat your smoker or slow cooker to 225°F (110°C).
2. Mix together paprika, garlic powder, brown sugar, cumin, salt, and pepper. Rub onto the pork shoulder.
3. Smoke the pork for about 8-10 hours, or cook in a slow cooker on low for 6-8 hours, until the pork is tender and easily pulled apart.
4. Once cooked, shred the pork with forks and mix with apple cider vinegar and BBQ sauce.
5. Serve on buns with coleslaw.

BBQ Chicken with Honey Mustard Glaze

Ingredients:

- 4 chicken breasts or thighs
- 1/2 cup honey
- 1/4 cup Dijon mustard
- 1 tablespoon apple cider vinegar
- Salt and pepper to taste

Instructions:

1. Preheat your grill to medium heat.
2. Season the chicken with salt and pepper.
3. In a small bowl, whisk together honey, Dijon mustard, and apple cider vinegar.
4. Grill the chicken for 6-7 minutes per side, basting with the honey mustard glaze during the last few minutes.
5. Serve hot with extra glaze on the side.

Grilled Shrimp Skewers with Cajun Spice

Ingredients:

- 1 lb large shrimp, peeled and deveined
- 2 tablespoons olive oil
- 2 tablespoons Cajun seasoning
- 1 tablespoon garlic powder
- 1/2 teaspoon cayenne pepper
- Salt and pepper to taste
- Lemon wedges (for serving)

Instructions:

1. Preheat the grill to medium-high heat.
2. In a bowl, toss the shrimp with olive oil, Cajun seasoning, garlic powder, cayenne pepper, salt, and pepper.
3. Thread the shrimp onto skewers and grill for 2-3 minutes per side until opaque and cooked through.
4. Serve with lemon wedges.

Spicy BBQ Pork Belly

Ingredients:

- 2 lbs pork belly, cut into cubes
- 1/4 cup soy sauce
- 2 tablespoons honey
- 1 tablespoon Sriracha sauce
- 1 tablespoon rice vinegar
- 1 teaspoon garlic powder
- 1 teaspoon ginger powder

Instructions:

1. Preheat your grill to medium-high heat.
2. In a bowl, whisk together soy sauce, honey, Sriracha, rice vinegar, garlic powder, and ginger powder.
3. Toss the pork belly cubes in the marinade and let sit for at least 30 minutes.
4. Grill the pork belly cubes for 5-7 minutes per side until crispy and cooked through.
5. Serve with your favorite dipping sauce.

Smoked Sausages with Beer and Mustard

Ingredients:

- 4 sausages (any variety you prefer)
- 1 cup beer
- 2 tablespoons Dijon mustard
- 1 tablespoon honey
- 1/2 teaspoon garlic powder
- Salt and pepper to taste

Instructions:

1. Preheat your smoker to 225°F (110°C).
2. Place the sausages in the smoker and cook for 2-3 hours, or until heated through.
3. In a saucepan, combine the beer, Dijon mustard, honey, garlic powder, salt, and pepper. Simmer for 10 minutes to reduce.
4. Serve the sausages with the beer mustard sauce.

Grilled Vegetables with Balsamic Glaze

Ingredients:

- 1 zucchini, sliced
- 1 bell pepper, sliced
- 1 red onion, sliced
- 1 cup cherry tomatoes
- 2 tablespoons olive oil
- Salt and pepper to taste
- 2 tablespoons balsamic glaze

Instructions:

1. Preheat the grill to medium heat.
2. Toss the vegetables in olive oil, salt, and pepper.
3. Grill the vegetables for 5-7 minutes per side, until tender and slightly charred.
4. Drizzle with balsamic glaze and serve.

BBQ Pulled Chicken Tacos

Ingredients:

- 4 chicken breasts
- 1/4 cup BBQ sauce
- 1 tablespoon olive oil
- 1 teaspoon cumin
- 1 teaspoon paprika
- 1 teaspoon garlic powder
- 1/2 teaspoon onion powder
- 1/4 teaspoon cayenne pepper
- 8 small tortillas
- 1 cup coleslaw (optional, for serving)
- Fresh cilantro, chopped (for garnish)

Instructions:

1. Preheat your oven to 375°F (190°C).
2. Season the chicken breasts with cumin, paprika, garlic powder, onion powder, cayenne, salt, and pepper.
3. In a skillet, heat olive oil over medium heat. Brown the chicken breasts for 2-3 minutes on each side.
4. Transfer the chicken to a baking dish and bake for 25-30 minutes or until fully cooked (165°F internal temperature).
5. Shred the chicken using two forks, then toss with BBQ sauce.
6. Warm the tortillas and fill with the pulled chicken, coleslaw, and cilantro.
7. Serve with extra BBQ sauce.

Smoky BBQ Meatballs

Ingredients:

- 1 lb ground beef or pork
- 1/2 cup breadcrumbs
- 1/4 cup grated Parmesan cheese
- 1/4 cup chopped parsley
- 1 egg
- 2 cloves garlic, minced
- 1 tablespoon smoked paprika
- 1 tablespoon BBQ sauce
- Salt and pepper to taste

Instructions:

1. Preheat your grill to medium heat.
2. In a large bowl, combine ground meat, breadcrumbs, Parmesan, parsley, egg, garlic, smoked paprika, BBQ sauce, salt, and pepper. Mix until well combined.
3. Form the mixture into 1-inch meatballs.
4. Grill the meatballs for 8-10 minutes, turning occasionally, until browned and cooked through (internal temperature should reach 160°F).
5. Serve with extra BBQ sauce for dipping.

Grilled Lamb Chops with Herb Marinade

Ingredients:

- 8 lamb chops
- 1/4 cup olive oil
- 2 tablespoons fresh rosemary, chopped
- 2 tablespoons fresh thyme, chopped
- 2 garlic cloves, minced
- Juice of 1 lemon
- Salt and pepper to taste

Instructions:

1. Preheat your grill to medium-high heat.
2. In a bowl, whisk together olive oil, rosemary, thyme, garlic, lemon juice, salt, and pepper.
3. Rub the marinade onto the lamb chops and let them sit for at least 30 minutes (or overnight in the fridge).
4. Grill the lamb chops for 4-5 minutes per side, until they reach your desired level of doneness (145°F for medium-rare).
5. Let the chops rest for a few minutes before serving.

BBQ Chicken Wings with Tangy Sauce

Ingredients:

- 12 chicken wings
- 1/4 cup BBQ sauce
- 1/4 cup hot sauce
- 2 tablespoons honey
- 1 tablespoon apple cider vinegar
- 1 teaspoon garlic powder
- Salt and pepper to taste

Instructions:

1. Preheat your grill to medium heat.
2. In a bowl, combine BBQ sauce, hot sauce, honey, apple cider vinegar, garlic powder, salt, and pepper.
3. Season the chicken wings with salt and pepper.
4. Grill the wings for 20-25 minutes, turning occasionally, until fully cooked and crispy.
5. Brush the wings with the tangy sauce during the last 5 minutes of grilling.
6. Serve with extra sauce on the side.

Cedar-Planked Salmon with Maple Glaze

Ingredients:

- 2 salmon fillets
- 1 cedar plank (soaked in water for 1 hour)
- 2 tablespoons maple syrup
- 1 tablespoon Dijon mustard
- 1 tablespoon soy sauce
- 1 teaspoon lemon juice
- Salt and pepper to taste

Instructions:

1. Preheat your grill to medium heat.
2. In a bowl, mix together maple syrup, Dijon mustard, soy sauce, lemon juice, salt, and pepper.
3. Place the salmon fillets on the soaked cedar plank.
4. Brush the maple glaze onto the salmon fillets.
5. Place the plank on the grill and cook for 15-20 minutes, or until the salmon flakes easily with a fork.
6. Serve the salmon with extra glaze.

BBQ Pulled Jackfruit Sandwiches

Ingredients:

- 2 cans young green jackfruit in brine, drained and shredded
- 1/4 cup BBQ sauce
- 1 tablespoon olive oil
- 1 onion, thinly sliced
- 1 teaspoon smoked paprika
- 1/2 teaspoon cumin
- Salt and pepper to taste
- 8 slider buns
- Coleslaw (for serving)

Instructions:

1. Preheat your grill to medium heat.
2. Heat olive oil in a skillet and sauté the onion until soft, about 5 minutes.
3. Add shredded jackfruit to the skillet, followed by smoked paprika, cumin, salt, pepper, and BBQ sauce. Stir well to combine.
4. Grill the jackfruit mixture in a foil packet for 15-20 minutes, stirring occasionally.
5. Serve the pulled jackfruit on slider buns with coleslaw.

Smoked Turkey Breast

Ingredients:

- 4-5 lb turkey breast
- 1/4 cup olive oil
- 1 tablespoon garlic powder
- 1 tablespoon onion powder
- 1 teaspoon smoked paprika
- Salt and pepper to taste
- Wood chips for smoking

Instructions:

1. Preheat your smoker to 225°F (110°C).
2. Rub the turkey breast with olive oil, garlic powder, onion powder, smoked paprika, salt, and pepper.
3. Place the turkey breast in the smoker and cook for about 4-5 hours, until the internal temperature reaches 165°F.
4. Let the turkey rest for 15 minutes before slicing.

Grilled Corn on the Cob with Chili Butter

Ingredients:

- 6 ears of corn, husked
- 1/4 cup unsalted butter, softened
- 1 tablespoon chili powder
- 1/2 teaspoon garlic powder
- Salt and pepper to taste
- Lime wedges (for serving)

Instructions:

1. Preheat your grill to medium-high heat.
2. In a small bowl, mix together the butter, chili powder, garlic powder, salt, and pepper.
3. Grill the corn for 10-12 minutes, turning occasionally, until lightly charred and tender.
4. Brush the grilled corn with chili butter and serve with lime wedges.

BBQ Beef Brisket Burnt Ends

Ingredients:

- 1 whole brisket, about 10 lbs
- 1/4 cup BBQ rub
- 1/2 cup BBQ sauce
- 1/4 cup honey
- 2 tablespoons apple cider vinegar

Instructions:

1. Preheat your smoker to 225°F (110°C).
2. Rub the brisket with BBQ rub and smoke for 8-10 hours, until the internal temperature reaches 195°F.
3. Cut the brisket into 1-inch cubes and toss with BBQ sauce, honey, and apple cider vinegar.
4. Smoke the burnt ends for an additional 2 hours, or until caramelized.
5. Serve with extra BBQ sauce.

Marinated Flank Steak with Chimichurri

Ingredients:

- 1 lb flank steak
- 1/4 cup olive oil
- 2 tablespoons red wine vinegar
- 2 cloves garlic, minced
- 1 teaspoon dried oregano
- 1 teaspoon cumin
- Salt and pepper to taste
- Chimichurri sauce (for serving)

Instructions:

1. Preheat your grill to high heat.
2. In a bowl, mix together olive oil, vinegar, garlic, oregano, cumin, salt, and pepper.
3. Marinate the flank steak in the mixture for at least 30 minutes (or overnight in the fridge).
4. Grill the flank steak for 4-5 minutes per side for medium-rare, or to your desired doneness.
5. Slice the steak against the grain and serve with chimichurri sauce.

Grilled Portobello Mushrooms with Garlic Butter

Ingredients:

- 4 large Portobello mushrooms
- 1/4 cup unsalted butter, melted
- 2 cloves garlic, minced
- 1 tablespoon fresh parsley, chopped
- Salt and pepper to taste
- Olive oil for grilling

Instructions:

1. Preheat your grill to medium heat.
2. Clean the Portobello mushrooms and remove the stems.
3. In a small bowl, mix together melted butter, garlic, parsley, salt, and pepper.
4. Brush the mushrooms with olive oil and grill for 5-7 minutes per side.
5. Once grilled, brush the mushrooms with garlic butter and serve immediately.

BBQ Baby Back Ribs with Dry Rub

Ingredients:

- 1 rack baby back ribs
- 1/4 cup brown sugar
- 1 tablespoon smoked paprika
- 1 tablespoon garlic powder
- 1 tablespoon onion powder
- 1 teaspoon salt
- 1 teaspoon black pepper
- 1 teaspoon cumin
- 1 teaspoon chili powder

Instructions:

1. Preheat your grill to indirect heat (275°F or 135°C).
2. Mix all dry rub ingredients in a bowl.
3. Remove the silver skin from the ribs and rub the dry rub all over the meat.
4. Place the ribs on the grill, bone side down, and cook for 2.5 to 3 hours, turning occasionally.
5. For the last 30 minutes, brush with your favorite BBQ sauce and cook until caramelized.
6. Slice and serve.

Smoked Whole Chicken with Lemon Herb Marinade

Ingredients:

- 1 whole chicken (about 4 lbs)
- 1/4 cup olive oil
- Juice and zest of 1 lemon
- 3 cloves garlic, minced
- 1 tablespoon fresh thyme, chopped
- 1 tablespoon fresh rosemary, chopped
- Salt and pepper to taste

Instructions:

1. Preheat your smoker to 225°F (110°C).
2. In a bowl, mix olive oil, lemon juice and zest, garlic, thyme, rosemary, salt, and pepper.
3. Rub the marinade all over the chicken and let it marinate for 1-2 hours (or overnight in the fridge).
4. Smoke the chicken for 3-4 hours, or until the internal temperature reaches 165°F in the thickest part of the thigh.
5. Rest for 10 minutes before serving.

BBQ Grilled Shrimp with Garlic Butter

Ingredients:

- 1 lb large shrimp, peeled and deveined
- 1/4 cup unsalted butter, melted
- 3 cloves garlic, minced
- 1 tablespoon fresh lemon juice
- 1 tablespoon fresh parsley, chopped
- Salt and pepper to taste
- Wooden skewers, soaked in water for 30 minutes

Instructions:

1. Preheat your grill to medium-high heat.
2. In a bowl, combine melted butter, garlic, lemon juice, parsley, salt, and pepper.
3. Thread the shrimp onto the soaked skewers and brush with the garlic butter mixture.
4. Grill for 2-3 minutes per side until the shrimp turn pink and are fully cooked.
5. Serve with extra garlic butter and a sprinkle of fresh parsley.

Grilled BBQ Chicken Thighs with Sweet Sauce

Ingredients:

- 6 bone-in, skin-on chicken thighs
- 1/4 cup BBQ sauce
- 2 tablespoons honey
- 1 tablespoon Dijon mustard
- 1 tablespoon olive oil
- Salt and pepper to taste

Instructions:

1. Preheat your grill to medium heat.
2. In a small bowl, combine BBQ sauce, honey, Dijon mustard, olive oil, salt, and pepper.
3. Season the chicken thighs with salt and pepper and grill for 5-7 minutes per side, or until the skin is crispy and the internal temperature reaches 165°F.
4. During the last 5 minutes of grilling, brush the thighs with the sweet BBQ sauce.
5. Serve with extra sauce on the side.

Spicy BBQ Meatloaf

Ingredients:

- 1 lb ground beef or pork
- 1/2 cup breadcrumbs
- 1/4 cup milk
- 1 egg
- 1/4 cup BBQ sauce
- 1 tablespoon hot sauce
- 1 tablespoon Worcestershire sauce
- 1/2 onion, finely chopped
- 1 teaspoon garlic powder
- Salt and pepper to taste

Instructions:

1. Preheat your grill to medium heat.
2. In a large bowl, combine ground meat, breadcrumbs, milk, egg, BBQ sauce, hot sauce, Worcestershire sauce, onion, garlic powder, salt, and pepper.
3. Form the mixture into a loaf shape and place it on a piece of foil.
4. Grill the meatloaf for 45-60 minutes, flipping occasionally, until the internal temperature reaches 160°F.
5. Let the meatloaf rest for 10 minutes before slicing.

Smoked Pork Shoulder with Apple Cider Glaze

Ingredients:

- 5-6 lb pork shoulder
- 1/4 cup apple cider vinegar
- 1/4 cup apple juice
- 1/4 cup brown sugar
- 2 tablespoons Dijon mustard
- 2 cloves garlic, minced
- Salt and pepper to taste

Instructions:

1. Preheat your smoker to 225°F (110°C).
2. Season the pork shoulder with salt and pepper.
3. Smoke the pork shoulder for 5-6 hours, or until it reaches an internal temperature of 190°F.
4. In the last 30 minutes of smoking, brush the pork with a glaze made of apple cider vinegar, apple juice, brown sugar, Dijon mustard, and garlic.
5. Let the pork rest for 10-15 minutes before shredding.

Grilled BBQ Tofu Skewers

Ingredients:

- 1 block firm tofu, pressed and cut into cubes
- 1/4 cup BBQ sauce
- 1 tablespoon olive oil
- 1 tablespoon soy sauce
- 1 teaspoon smoked paprika
- Salt and pepper to taste
- Wooden skewers, soaked in water for 30 minutes

Instructions:

1. Preheat your grill to medium-high heat.
2. In a bowl, mix BBQ sauce, olive oil, soy sauce, smoked paprika, salt, and pepper.
3. Toss the tofu cubes in the marinade and let sit for 15-20 minutes.
4. Thread the tofu onto the skewers and grill for 4-5 minutes per side, until grill marks appear.
5. Serve with extra BBQ sauce for dipping.

Cajun-Style BBQ Shrimp

Ingredients:

- 1 lb shrimp, peeled and deveined
- 2 tablespoons Cajun seasoning
- 1 tablespoon olive oil
- 1 tablespoon lemon juice
- 1 tablespoon chopped parsley
- Salt and pepper to taste

Instructions:

1. Preheat your grill to medium-high heat.
2. In a bowl, combine Cajun seasoning, olive oil, lemon juice, salt, and pepper.
3. Toss the shrimp in the seasoning mixture and grill for 2-3 minutes per side.
4. Garnish with chopped parsley and serve with lemon wedges.

BBQ Sliders with Pickles and Mustard

Ingredients:

- 1 lb ground beef
- 1 tablespoon BBQ sauce
- 1 tablespoon mustard
- 12 slider buns
- Pickles for topping
- Salt and pepper to taste

Instructions:

1. Preheat your grill to medium heat.
2. Season the ground beef with salt, pepper, and BBQ sauce, and form into small patties.
3. Grill the sliders for 3-4 minutes per side until cooked through.
4. Assemble the sliders by placing a patty on each bun, topping with mustard and pickles.
5. Serve immediately with your favorite sides.

Grilled Fish Tacos with BBQ Sauce

Ingredients:

- 1 lb white fish fillets (like tilapia or cod)
- 1 tablespoon olive oil
- Salt and pepper to taste
- 1/4 cup BBQ sauce
- 8 small corn tortillas
- 1/2 cup cabbage, shredded
- 1/4 cup cilantro, chopped
- 1 tablespoon lime juice
- 1/4 cup sour cream

Instructions:

1. Preheat your grill to medium-high heat.
2. Brush the fish fillets with olive oil and season with salt and pepper.
3. Grill the fish for 3-4 minutes per side, until cooked through and flaky.
4. While the fish is grilling, warm the tortillas on the grill for 1 minute on each side.
5. Once the fish is done, brush with BBQ sauce and flake it into pieces.
6. Assemble the tacos by placing fish on each tortilla and topping with shredded cabbage, cilantro, lime juice, and a dollop of sour cream.

Smoked Beef Short Ribs

Ingredients:

- 4 beef short ribs (about 3 lbs)
- 1/4 cup brown sugar
- 2 tablespoons paprika
- 1 tablespoon garlic powder
- 1 tablespoon onion powder
- 1 tablespoon black pepper
- 1 tablespoon salt
- 1 teaspoon cumin
- 1 teaspoon chili powder
- 1/4 cup apple cider vinegar
- 1/4 cup water

Instructions:

1. Preheat your smoker to 225°F (110°C).
2. Mix the brown sugar, paprika, garlic powder, onion powder, black pepper, salt, cumin, and chili powder in a bowl to create the rub.
3. Rub the seasoning mixture generously onto the short ribs.
4. Place the ribs in the smoker and cook for 6-8 hours, until the internal temperature reaches 200°F.
5. During the last hour of smoking, mix apple cider vinegar and water, then spritz the ribs every 30 minutes.
6. Once done, let the ribs rest for 10-15 minutes before slicing and serving.

Grilled Honey BBQ Chicken Drumsticks

Ingredients:

- 10 chicken drumsticks
- 1/4 cup honey
- 1/4 cup BBQ sauce
- 1 tablespoon soy sauce
- 1 tablespoon olive oil
- Salt and pepper to taste

Instructions:

1. Preheat your grill to medium heat.
2. In a bowl, whisk together honey, BBQ sauce, soy sauce, olive oil, salt, and pepper.
3. Coat the drumsticks with the marinade and let them marinate for 30 minutes.
4. Grill the drumsticks for 20-25 minutes, turning occasionally, until the internal temperature reaches 165°F and the skin is crispy.
5. Serve with extra BBQ sauce on the side.

BBQ Duck with Sweet Soy Glaze

Ingredients:

- 2 duck breasts
- 1/4 cup soy sauce
- 2 tablespoons honey
- 2 tablespoons rice vinegar
- 1 tablespoon sesame oil
- 1 clove garlic, minced
- 1 tablespoon ginger, grated

Instructions:

1. Preheat your grill to medium heat.
2. In a small bowl, whisk together soy sauce, honey, rice vinegar, sesame oil, garlic, and ginger to create the glaze.
3. Score the duck breasts and season with salt and pepper.
4. Grill the duck for 5-7 minutes per side, basting with the glaze.
5. Let the duck rest for 5 minutes before slicing and serving.

Grilled Zucchini and Squash with Smoky Sauce

Ingredients:

- 2 zucchinis, sliced into rounds
- 2 yellow squashes, sliced into rounds
- 2 tablespoons olive oil
- 1 tablespoon smoked paprika
- 1 tablespoon garlic powder
- Salt and pepper to taste

Instructions:

1. Preheat your grill to medium heat.
2. Toss the zucchini and squash slices with olive oil, smoked paprika, garlic powder, salt, and pepper.
3. Grill the vegetables for 3-4 minutes per side until tender and slightly charred.
4. Serve immediately with a drizzle of extra smoky sauce, if desired.

BBQ-Style Pulled Beef Sandwiches

Ingredients:

- 3 lb beef chuck roast
- 1 tablespoon paprika
- 1 tablespoon garlic powder
- 1 tablespoon onion powder
- 1 teaspoon cumin
- 1 teaspoon smoked paprika
- Salt and pepper to taste
- 1/2 cup BBQ sauce
- 8 sandwich buns
- Pickles for topping

Instructions:

1. Preheat your grill or smoker to 225°F (110°C).
2. Season the beef roast with paprika, garlic powder, onion powder, cumin, smoked paprika, salt, and pepper.
3. Smoke the beef roast for 4-5 hours, until it reaches an internal temperature of 190°F.
4. Shred the beef using two forks and mix with BBQ sauce.
5. Serve on sandwich buns with pickles on top.

Grilled Pineapple with Brown Sugar Glaze

Ingredients:

- 1 pineapple, peeled, cored, and cut into rings
- 1/4 cup brown sugar
- 1 tablespoon butter, melted
- 1/4 teaspoon cinnamon

Instructions:

1. Preheat your grill to medium heat.
2. In a small bowl, mix together brown sugar, melted butter, and cinnamon.
3. Brush the pineapple rings with the glaze and grill for 3-4 minutes per side until caramelized.
4. Serve immediately as a side dish or dessert.

BBQ Brisket Tacos with Spicy Salsa

Ingredients:

- 2 lb brisket
- 1 tablespoon chili powder
- 1 tablespoon cumin
- 1 tablespoon garlic powder
- Salt and pepper to taste
- 8 small tortillas
- 1/2 cup spicy salsa
- Fresh cilantro for garnish

Instructions:

1. Preheat your smoker to 225°F (110°C).
2. Season the brisket with chili powder, cumin, garlic powder, salt, and pepper.
3. Smoke the brisket for 6-8 hours, until the internal temperature reaches 200°F.
4. Slice the brisket thinly and assemble tacos with brisket, spicy salsa, and fresh cilantro on tortillas.
5. Serve immediately.

Smoked Salmon with Dill and Lemon

Ingredients:

- 2 salmon fillets
- 2 tablespoons olive oil
- Salt and pepper to taste
- 1 tablespoon fresh dill, chopped
- 1 lemon, sliced

Instructions:

1. Preheat your smoker to 225°F (110°C).
2. Season the salmon with olive oil, salt, and pepper.
3. Smoke the salmon for 1-2 hours, until the internal temperature reaches 145°F.
4. Garnish with fresh dill and lemon slices before serving.

BBQ Veggie Skewers with Herb Marinade

Ingredients:

- 1 zucchini, sliced into thick rounds
- 1 bell pepper, chopped into chunks
- 1 red onion, chopped into chunks
- 8 oz mushrooms, whole or halved
- 1 cup cherry tomatoes
- 1/4 cup olive oil
- 2 tablespoons balsamic vinegar
- 1 tablespoon fresh rosemary, chopped
- 1 tablespoon fresh thyme, chopped
- 2 cloves garlic, minced
- Salt and pepper to taste

Instructions:

1. Preheat your grill to medium heat.
2. In a bowl, whisk together olive oil, balsamic vinegar, rosemary, thyme, garlic, salt, and pepper.
3. Thread the vegetables onto skewers, alternating types of veggies.
4. Brush the skewers with the herb marinade.
5. Grill for 6-8 minutes, turning occasionally, until the veggies are tender and slightly charred.
6. Serve immediately.

Grilled BBQ Pork Chops with Apple Sauce

Ingredients:

- 4 bone-in pork chops
- Salt and pepper to taste
- 1/2 cup BBQ sauce
- 1/2 cup apple sauce
- 1 tablespoon honey
- 1/2 teaspoon ground cinnamon

Instructions:

1. Preheat your grill to medium heat.
2. Season the pork chops with salt and pepper on both sides.
3. Grill the pork chops for 5-7 minutes per side until the internal temperature reaches 145°F.
4. While grilling, mix the BBQ sauce, apple sauce, honey, and cinnamon in a bowl.
5. During the last 2 minutes of grilling, brush the pork chops with the apple BBQ sauce.
6. Serve with extra apple sauce on the side.

Smoked Brisket Chili

Ingredients:

- 2 lbs smoked brisket, shredded
- 1 onion, chopped
- 2 cloves garlic, minced
- 1 can (15 oz) kidney beans, drained and rinsed
- 1 can (15 oz) black beans, drained and rinsed
- 1 can (15 oz) diced tomatoes
- 1 tablespoon chili powder
- 1 teaspoon cumin
- 1/2 teaspoon paprika
- Salt and pepper to taste
- 2 cups beef broth

Instructions:

1. In a large pot, sauté onion and garlic over medium heat until softened.
2. Add the shredded smoked brisket and stir to combine.
3. Add beans, diced tomatoes, chili powder, cumin, paprika, salt, and pepper.
4. Pour in the beef broth and bring the chili to a simmer.
5. Let it cook for 30-40 minutes, stirring occasionally.
6. Serve hot with optional toppings like sour cream or shredded cheese.

Grilled Shrimp with Pineapple Salsa

Ingredients:

- 1 lb large shrimp, peeled and deveined
- 1 tablespoon olive oil
- Salt and pepper to taste
- 1 cup fresh pineapple, diced
- 1/4 cup red onion, finely chopped
- 1 tablespoon fresh cilantro, chopped
- 1 tablespoon lime juice
- 1/2 teaspoon jalapeño, finely chopped (optional)

Instructions:

1. Preheat your grill to medium-high heat.
2. Toss the shrimp in olive oil, salt, and pepper.
3. Grill the shrimp for 2-3 minutes per side until they are opaque and cooked through.
4. While grilling, mix the pineapple, red onion, cilantro, lime juice, and jalapeño in a bowl to make the salsa.
5. Serve the grilled shrimp with the pineapple salsa on top.

BBQ Hot Dogs with Spicy Relish

Ingredients:

- 4 beef or pork hot dogs
- 4 hot dog buns
- 1/2 cup spicy mustard
- 1/4 cup relish
- 1 tablespoon jalapeño, finely chopped (optional)
- 1 tablespoon ketchup (optional)

Instructions:

1. Preheat your grill to medium heat.
2. Grill the hot dogs for 5-7 minutes, turning occasionally until evenly cooked.
3. While grilling, mix spicy mustard, relish, jalapeño, and ketchup (if using) in a bowl.
4. Place the grilled hot dogs in buns and top with the spicy relish mixture.
5. Serve immediately.

Grilled Baby Potatoes with Smoky Ranch Dressing

Ingredients:

- 1 lb baby potatoes, halved
- 2 tablespoons olive oil
- Salt and pepper to taste
- 1 tablespoon smoked paprika
- 1/2 cup ranch dressing
- 1 teaspoon fresh parsley, chopped (optional)

Instructions:

1. Preheat your grill to medium heat.
2. Toss the baby potatoes with olive oil, salt, pepper, and smoked paprika.
3. Grill the potatoes for 15-20 minutes, turning occasionally until tender and crispy.
4. Drizzle with ranch dressing and garnish with fresh parsley.
5. Serve immediately.

BBQ Beef Kabobs with Vegetables

Ingredients:

- 1 lb beef sirloin, cut into 1-inch cubes
- 1 bell pepper, cut into chunks
- 1 red onion, cut into chunks
- 1 zucchini, sliced
- 1/4 cup olive oil
- 1/4 cup soy sauce
- 1 tablespoon Worcestershire sauce
- 2 cloves garlic, minced
- 1 teaspoon dried oregano
- Salt and pepper to taste

Instructions:

1. Preheat your grill to medium heat.
2. In a bowl, combine olive oil, soy sauce, Worcestershire sauce, garlic, oregano, salt, and pepper.
3. Toss the beef cubes and vegetables in the marinade and let it sit for 30 minutes.
4. Thread the beef and vegetables onto skewers, alternating between beef and veggies.
5. Grill the kabobs for 3-4 minutes per side until the beef is cooked to your preferred doneness.
6. Serve immediately.

Grilled Shrimp Po' Boys

Ingredients:

- 1 lb large shrimp, peeled and deveined
- 1 tablespoon olive oil
- 1 teaspoon Cajun seasoning
- 4 soft baguette rolls or Po' Boy rolls
- 1/2 cup shredded lettuce
- 1/2 cup sliced tomatoes
- 1/4 cup pickles, sliced
- 1/4 cup mayonnaise
- 1 tablespoon Dijon mustard
- 1 teaspoon lemon juice
- Hot sauce, to taste

Instructions:

1. Preheat your grill to medium-high heat.
2. Toss the shrimp with olive oil and Cajun seasoning.
3. Grill the shrimp for 2-3 minutes per side until pink and cooked through.
4. In a small bowl, mix mayonnaise, Dijon mustard, lemon juice, and hot sauce to make a spicy sauce.
5. Split the rolls and spread the spicy sauce on both sides.
6. Layer shredded lettuce, sliced tomatoes, pickles, and grilled shrimp in the rolls.
7. Serve immediately.

Smoked Beef Tenderloin with Red Wine Sauce

Ingredients:

- 2 lb beef tenderloin, trimmed
- 1 tablespoon olive oil
- Salt and pepper to taste
- 2 tablespoons butter
- 1 shallot, finely chopped
- 1 cup red wine
- 1 cup beef broth
- 2 teaspoons fresh thyme leaves

Instructions:

1. Preheat your smoker to 225°F.
2. Rub the beef tenderloin with olive oil, salt, and pepper.
3. Smoke the beef tenderloin for 2-3 hours, or until it reaches an internal temperature of 125°F for medium-rare.
4. In a saucepan, melt butter and sauté shallots until softened.
5. Add red wine, beef broth, and thyme. Simmer for 10-15 minutes until the sauce thickens.
6. Remove the beef tenderloin from the smoker, let it rest for 10 minutes, then slice.
7. Serve the beef slices with the red wine sauce.

Grilled Cajun Chicken with Avocado Salsa

Ingredients:

- 4 boneless, skinless chicken breasts
- 2 tablespoons Cajun seasoning
- 1 tablespoon olive oil
- 1 ripe avocado, diced
- 1/4 cup red onion, finely chopped
- 1/4 cup fresh cilantro, chopped
- 1 tablespoon lime juice
- Salt and pepper to taste

Instructions:

1. Preheat your grill to medium-high heat.
2. Rub the chicken breasts with Cajun seasoning and olive oil.
3. Grill the chicken for 5-6 minutes per side, or until cooked through (internal temperature of 165°F).
4. In a bowl, mix diced avocado, red onion, cilantro, lime juice, salt, and pepper to make the salsa.
5. Serve the grilled chicken topped with avocado salsa.

BBQ Grilled Flatbreads with Veggies

Ingredients:

- 2 flatbreads or naan bread
- 1/2 cup olive oil
- 1 zucchini, sliced thinly
- 1 bell pepper, sliced
- 1 red onion, sliced
- 1 cup cherry tomatoes, halved
- 1/2 cup crumbled feta cheese
- Salt and pepper to taste
- 1 teaspoon dried oregano

Instructions:

1. Preheat your grill to medium heat.
2. Brush the flatbreads with olive oil and season with salt, pepper, and oregano.
3. Grill the flatbreads for 2-3 minutes on each side until lightly toasted.
4. In a grill basket or foil packet, grill the vegetables for 5-7 minutes until tender and slightly charred.
5. Remove the flatbreads from the grill and top with the grilled vegetables and crumbled feta cheese.
6. Serve immediately.

Smoked Salmon with BBQ Glaze

Ingredients:

- 2 fillets of salmon
- 1/4 cup BBQ sauce
- 1 tablespoon honey
- 1 tablespoon Dijon mustard
- 1 teaspoon lemon juice
- Fresh dill for garnish

Instructions:

1. Preheat your smoker to 225°F.
2. Mix BBQ sauce, honey, Dijon mustard, and lemon juice to create the glaze.
3. Coat the salmon fillets with the glaze.
4. Smoke the salmon for 1-1.5 hours until it reaches an internal temperature of 145°F and the fish is flakey.
5. Garnish with fresh dill and serve immediately.

www.ingramcontent.com/pod-product-compliance
Lightning Source LLC
LaVergne TN
LVHW081341060526
838201LV00055B/2789

9 7 9 8 3 4 8 4 6 3 9 2 2